BELONGS TO

_____
_____
_____

GOLF

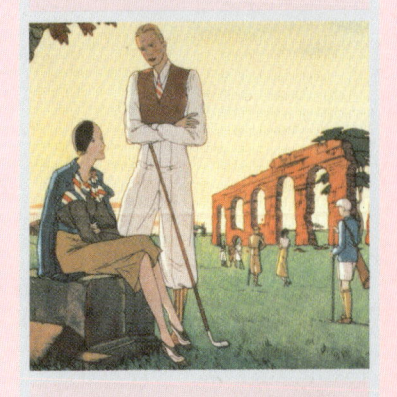

IN WORDS AND PICTURES

JARROLD
PUBLISHING

GOLF

Golf for most of us is just another method of beating around the bush.

HERBERT V. PROCHNOW

Playing the game I have learned the meaning of humility. It has given me an understanding of the futility of human effort.

ABBA EBAN

Golf is so popular simply because it is the best game in the world at which to be bad.

A.A. MILNE

The least thing upset him on the links. He missed short putts because of the uproar of butterflies in the adjoining meadow.

P.G. WODEHOUSE

GOLF

FRONTISPIECE OF R. CLARK'S
"GOLF – A ROYAL AND ANCIENT GAME"
Clark Stanton 1832–1894

GOLF

JOHN WHYTE MELVILLE OF BENNOCHY AND STRATHKINNESS
Sir Francis Grant 1803–1878

GOLF

A golf spectator is satisfied when he gets to see, at least a few times during the course of his long day, a ball struck with consummate power and amazing control; a ball sent soaring from a standing start, then floating to earth and stopping within a prescribed swatch of lawn. It is an awesome sensation, not unlike watching a rocket launch.

AL BARKOW

Show me a man whose feet are firmly planted on solid ground, and I'll show you a man about to try a difficult putt.

HERBERT V. PROCHNOW

If a woman can walk, she can play golf.

LOUISE SUGGS

GOLF

Every great golfer has learned to think positively, to assume the success and not the failure of a shot, to disregard misfortune and to accept disaster, and never to indulge the futility of remorse and blame. These are the hardest lessons of all.

PAT WARD-THOMAS

Golfers are the greatest worriers in the world of sports....In fast-action sports, like football, baseball, basketball, or tennis, there is little time to worry compared to the time a golfer has on his hands between shots.

BILLY CASPER

GOLF

GOLFING AT WESTWARD HO!
Francis Powell Hopkins 1830–1913

GOLF

The Coarse Golfer: one who has to shout "Fore" when he putts.

MICHAEL GREEN

Golf is a good walk spoiled.

MARK TWAIN

Golf is a game where you sock the ball hard and walk four feet.

HERBERT V. PROCHNOW

Golf is an ideal diversion, but a ruinous disease.

B.C. FORBES

It is nothing new or original to say that golf is played one stroke at a time. But it took me many years to realise it.

BOBBY JONES

GOLF

SPORTS: GOLF 1900

Christa Kieffer

GOLF

A TOUR IN ITALY − ROMAN CAMPAGNA, WITH GOLFERS
Edina-Vittorio Accornero

GOLF

If you watch a game, it's fun. If you play it, it's recreation. If you work at it, it's golf.

BOB HOPE

A teacher was taking her first golf lesson.

"Is the word spelled 'put' or 'putt'?" she asked the instructor.

"'Putt' is correct," he replied. "'Put' means to place a thing where you want it. 'Putt' means a vain attempt to do the same thing."

HERBERT V. PROCHNOW

GOLF

THE FIFTH TEE, ST. ANDREWS, 1921
John Sutton

GOLF

Golfers don't need to diet. They live on greens.

If you can't break 85 you have no business on the golf course. If you can break 85 you probably have no business.

Farmer's Almanac

A noted psychologist's wife asked him why he never let her play golf with him. "My dear," he admonished her, "there are three things a man must do alone: Testify, die, and putt."

BENNETT CERF

Anyone who thinks our country is out of the woods should visit a golf course on a weekend.

HERBERT V. PROCHNOW

GOLF

Golf is essentially an exercise in masochism conducted out of doors: it affords opportunity for a certain swank, it induces a sense of kinship in its victims, and it forces them to breathe fresh air, but it is, at bottom, an elaborate and addictive rite calculated to drive them crazy for hours on end and send them straight to the whisky bottle after that.

PAUL O'NEIL

The best part of golf is that if you observe the etiquette, you can always find a game. I don't care how good you play, you can find somebody who can beat you, and I don't care how bad you play, you can find somebody you can beat.

HARVEY PENICK

They say if you drink, don't drive.... I don't even putt.

I know I'm getting better at golf because I'm hitting fewer spectators.

GERALD R. FORD

GOLF

THE FIRST GREEN ST. ANDREWS, 1798

GOLFING – IN SOUTHERN ENGLAND AND THE CONTINENT
Published by the Southern Railway

GOLF

I must go down to the links again,
To the rolling links and the sand,
And all I ask is a new ball
And a club to fit my hand.

MARCUS DODS

Handicap: an allocation of strokes on one or more holes that permits two golfers of very different ability to do equally poorly on the same course.

HENRY BEARD
AND ROY McKIE

At least he can't cheat on his score — because all you have to do is look back down the fairway and count the wounded.

BOB HOPE

Fairway: the well-kept and seldom used portion of a golf course.

GOLF

Golf: a game in which you claim the privileges of age, and retain the playthings of childhood.

SAMUEL JOHNSON

Golfball: a sphere made of rubber bands wound up about half as tensely as the man trying to hit it.

Golf is like eating soup with a fork – you can't get enough of it.

Golf is like marriage – it looks so easy to those who haven't tried it.

Great golfers are born. Good golfers are made.

GOLF

THE GOLFERS
Charles Lees 1800–1880

GOLF

Hole-in-one: an occurrence in which a ball is hit directly from the tee into the hole on a single shot by a golfer playing alone.

HENRY BEARD AND ROY McKIE

I'd like to see the fairways more narrow. Then everybody would have to play from the rough, not just me.

SEVE BALLESTEROS

I don't know a thing about golf. Why, if I wanted to hit a ball I wouldn't know which end of the caddy to take hold of!

ALAN CROFTS

GOLF

HARPER'S MAGAZINE, APRIL 1898

GOLF

ALL SQUARE AND ONE TO PLAY, THE EARLY DAYS OF GOLF
George Hillyard Swinstead 1860–1926

GOLF

It is almost impossible to remember how tragic a place the world is when one is playing golf.

MARK TWAIN

The secret of missing a tree is to aim straight at it.

MICHAEL GREEN

If your ball chance to land in a bunker or whins,
Don't lay the fault to account of your sins;
Just think that it got there, without any doubt,
That you might show your skill in getting it out.

DON LEWIS

GOLF

LA VIE PARISIENNE, 1922

GOLF

Par: mathematical perfection, usually attained with a soft pencil and not-so-soft conscience.

Remember the maxim for all you are worth,
If you scuff with your iron, you put back the turf.

ROYAL DORNOCH GOLF CLUB ROOM

It's still good sportsmanship to not pick up lost balls while they are still rolling.

MARK TWAIN

ALSO IN THIS SERIES

Cats – In Words and Pictures
Dogs – In Words and Pictures
Women – In Words and Pictures

ALSO AVAILABLE

In Praise of Happiness
In Praise of Friends
In Praise of Mothers
In Praise of Children

First published in Great Britain in 1996 by
JARROLD PUBLISHING LTD
Whitefriars, Norwich NR3 1TR

Developed and produced by
FOUR SEASONS PUBLISHING LTD
1 Durrington Avenue, London SW20 8NT

Text research by *Pauline Barrett*
Designed in association with *The Bridgewater Book Company*
Edited by *David Notley* and *Peter Bridgewater*
Picture research by *Vanessa Fletcher*
Printed in Dubai

Copyright © 1996 Four Seasons Publishing Ltd

All rights reserved.

ISBN 0-7117-0869-X

ACKNOWLEDGEMENTS

Four Seasons Publishing Ltd would like to thank all those
who kindly gave permission to reproduce the words and visual
material in this book; copyright holders have been identified
where possible and we apologise for any inadvertent omissions.

We would particularly like to thank the following
for the use of pictures: *Bridgeman Art Library,
Christie's Images, The Image Bank.*

Front Cover THE TRIUMVIRATE J.H. TAYLOR,
JAMES BRAID AND HARRY VARDON GOLF CHAMPIONS, *Clement Flower*
Title Page: A TOUR IN ITALY – ROMAN CAMPAGNA,
WITH GOLFERS, *Edina-Vittorio Accornero*
Endpaper: THE GOLFERS, *Charles Lees 1800–1880*
Frontispiece and Back Cover: CHICAGO TRIBUNE COVER 11 JUNE 1922 –
PORTRAIT OF A WOMAN GOLFER, *Maude Martin Ellis*